C000089100

The purpose of this study guide is to provide supplemental educational material. It is not intended as a substitute or replacement of AN UNSUITABLE JOB FOR A WOMAN.

Published by SuperSummary, www.supersummary.com

ISBN – 9798616297822

For more information or to learn about our complete library of study guides, please visit http://www.supersummary.com

Please submit any comments, corrections, or questions to:
http://www.supersummary.com/support/

TABLE OF CONTENTS

P.D. James wrote four detective novels centered on Inspector Adam Dalgliesh before publishing *An Unsuitable Job for a Woman* featuring protagonist and private investigator Cordelia Gray, with the popular character Dalgliesh making a cameo appearance. The novel was published in 1972 and is set at the same time, in the city of London.

While this book is faithful to many tropes of the genre, it is notable for James's elegant prose and detailed descriptions, as well as her interest in the inner workings of the human mind. James's characters are complicated but their motives are simple; the storyline is complex but, once teased out, reveals a straightforward series of events.

The book reflects an intellectual curiosity about the relationships between parents and children, between nature and nurture, and the disparity that can exist between appearance and reality. Writing in the close third person, James sometimes blurs the lines between her characters' thoughts and the narrator's perspective, using rhetorical questions to invite the reader to consider plot as well as more esoteric themes like love, right versus wrong, and intended and unintended consequences.

P.D. James published under her initials as it was unusual for a woman to write detective fiction. The novel overtly addresses the ways women are often underestimated and shunted aside. Cordelia uses her femininity as an asset, but her mind allows her to crack the case, specifically her intellect and ability to follow logic and reason over emotion. In ironic contrast, the male characters are less able to contain their emotions. This is a story about secrets, lies, family, the fine line between criminals and those who catch them, and how "it isn't what you suspect, it's what you can prove that counts" (87).

Plot Summary

The novel follows many conventions of detective fiction, beginning with a seemingly unsolvable crime, which in this case is not a crime at all. A young man, Mark Callender, committed suicide. His father, Sir Ronald Callender, wants to hire a private detective to find out why. He intends to hire Bernie Pryde, a former police officer, but instead gets Bernie's partner Cordelia Gray, who recently became the sole proprietor of the agency after Bernie's own suicide. Bernie left a note explaining he had been diagnosed with cancer; Mark's suicide is less easily explained.

Though she is often met with skepticism, due to her gender and her youth, Cordelia follows the investigative protocol she learned from Bernie. She starts by visiting the cottage where Mark died. Several incongruities there arouse her curiosity, and she follows these clues and those that follow, ultimately discovering that Mark did not commit suicide: He was murdered.

Cordelia also discovers that Mark's biological mother was Elizabeth Leaming, whom he knew as his father's secretary/assistant. Miss Leaming conspired with Sir Ronald and his wife, Evelyn, to pretend the baby was Evelyn's so that Evelyn's wealthy father would not cut her out of his will. Evelyn was unable to have a child of her own and was motivated to go along with this conspiracy in hopes of finally gaining her father's approval; Sir Ronald wanted to avoid scandal and, as he grew up poor, to obtain his wife's inheritance.

Three days before her death, when Mark was nine months old, Evelyn asked her old nanny to secret away her prayer book and give it to Mark when he turned 21. In that prayer book she left a coded message with her blood type. When Mark found that message, he realized she was not his biological mother. Being a man of principle, he told his father he would not accept his inheritance or the lifestyle it allowed him, as it was obtained through deception. Mark left Cambridge and took a job as a gardener on an estate, moving into a rustic cottage on the grounds.

Sir Ronald was upset and angered by Mark's actions, afraid that his secret would get out and—more importantly—that his professional reputation and the financial backing for his laboratory were in danger. Mark's renunciation was particularly galling because Sir Ronald was born poor, as a lowly gardener on his future in-laws' estate. Sir Ronald killed Mark and staged the scene to suggest an accidental death due to autoerotic asphyxiation. He dressed his son in women's lingerie, applied lipstick to his mouth, and left pages from a pornographic magazine on the table. Sir Ronald used his faithful laboratory assistant, Chris Lunn, to fabricate an alibi. But to Sir Ronald's surprise, when Mark was discovered dead, his face was cleaned of lipstick, the pornography was gone, he was dressed in his own clothes, and someone had left a suicide note. The inquest ruled Mark's death a suicide. Sir Ronald hires Cordelia, ostensibly to discover his son's motivation for suicide but really to find out who interceded after the murder.

Cordelia discovers that some of Mark's college friends found his body and planned to cover up the suggestion of sexual experimentation gone wrong, but before they could do so, Miss Leaming came on the scene and did the job herself—though she did not realize Mark had been murdered by his own father. Sir Ronald has Chris Lunn follow Cordelia to keep an eye on her investigation, and Lunn tries to kill her; she escapes his plan, and he is killed fleeing her revenge. Cordelia confronts Sir Ronald, and Miss Leaming overhears their conversation; when Miss Leaming realizes Sir Ronald killed their son, she shoots him dead.

Cordelia and Miss Leaming stage Sir Ronald's death as a suicide and concoct a story for the police. Their plan succeeds, then Cordelia is summoned by New Scotland Yard to meet with Chief Superintendent Adam Dalgliesh, who is suspicious of her story and the circumstances of Sir Ronald's death. Cordelia nearly breaks down under his interrogation but forces herself to adhere to the principles her mentor Bernie Pryde taught her, rules that came from the superintendent himself. Dalgliesh knows she is lying but can't prove it, and only in the last pages of the novel does he realize his own teachings and techniques are being used against him. Dalgliesh had fired Bernie from the police many years before, and in the end Dalgliesh "find[s] it ironic and oddly satisfying that Pryde took his revenge" (250) by training Cordelia so well that she outwits him. The novel ends with Cordelia finding a prospective client waiting outside her office door, signaling her success and setting the stage for further novels.

CHAPTER SUMMARIES AND ANALYSES

Chapter 1

Chapter 1 Summary

One June morning, Cordelia Gray arrives at the detective agency office she co-owns with former police officer Bernie Pryde and discovers he has locked himself in his office and slit his wrists. He has left her a note apologizing and explaining he was diagnosed with cancer; he has also left her his half of their failing business, emphasizing "*all* the equipment*" (16), which she realizes is a coded message to remind her to take possession of an illegal gun and three bullets. Cordelia secrets these away then notifies the police of Bernie's death.

Bernie, like Cordelia, does not have any relatives, so she cleans out his office and his home, where she finds "the sad detritus of a solitary and mismanaged life" (28). Cordelia discovers the agency is on the verge of going under and that Bernie did not own the house where he rented her a room, leaving her virtually homeless and on the verge of bankruptcy. She resolves to keep the agency afloat as long as she can, though she has little optimism.

Cordelia returns from being the solitary mourner at Bernie's cremation to find Elizabeth Leaming waiting at the office door. When Miss Leaming learns Bernie is dead she prepares to leave, but Cordelia begs her to stay. Miss Leaming consults with her employer, semi-famous microbiologist Sir Ronald Callender, who agrees to consider Cordelia for the job. Cordelia and Miss Leaming take the train to Cambridge to meet him.

6

They are met at the station by Chris Lunn, and Cordelia wonders at the various roles played by Miss Leaming and Lunn, speculating that they both might be more than they appear. She is introduced to Sir Richard Callender, who explains that his 21-year-old son, Mark Callender, recently left Cambridge, where he had been studying history, to take a job as a gardener. Then, 18 days into this new life, he hung himself with a leather strap.

Sir Richard wants a detective to find out why Mark killed himself, as the suicide note left was just a passage from William Blake's *The Marriage of Heaven and Hell*. Miss Leaming opposes this investigation, saying, "This lust always to know! It's only prying. If he'd wanted us to know, he'd have told us" (42). Sir Ronald insists he wants to know if someone, even if that someone was himself, was responsible.

Cordelia interviews Sir Ronald and Miss Leaming, learning that Mark's mother died when he was a baby and that he was sent to a succession of boarding schools; he was due to inherit a "considerable fortune" (43) from his maternal grandfather in just a few years' time. Mark was healthy and gave no indication for why he left Cambridge or why he took a job as a gardener. Miss Leaming again grows agitated at the prospect of digging into Mark's life, but Sir Ronald is insistent. He provides names for two of Mark's friends, siblings Hugo and Sophie Tilling; a letter authorizing Cordelia to ask questions on his behalf; and a picture of Mark that Miss Leaming took a year before. After a slightly awkward and strange dinner with Callender, his team of scientists, Miss Leaming, and Lunn, Cordelia returns by train to London. Studying the photograph, Cordelia considers that she has learned very little about Mark's life or his death, and that all the picture tells her is that "for one recorded second at least, he had known how to be happy" (51).

Chapter 1 Analysis

In detective fiction private eyes are traditionally loners who follow their own code. They are usually terse, withdrawn men with tragic backstories and an air of dissolution. In making her protagonist a pretty young woman, P.D. James subverts some of the genre's tropes while still writing a traditional detective story.

Cordelia is presented as a sympathetic figure though not a tragic one. Bernie is the character to be pitied, the kind of person who leaves behind "thick woolen combinations [underwear] felted with machine washing and stained brown about the crotch" (28). He was fired from "the only job he had ever wanted to do" (30), though he had been too proud to tell Cordelia he'd been kicked off the force. When Cordelia learns about it after his death, she blames Adam Dalgliesh, Bernie's former supervisor, for the resultant unhappiness of Bernie's life. In demonstration of her resiliency, she sees Bernie's suicide as a reason she must keep the agency open. Determination is one of her defining characteristics.

James won renown for her Dalgliesh novels before publishing *An Unsuitable Job for a Woman,* and by connecting him to Cordelia she is endowing her with some of Dalgliesh's legitimacy, both as a character and in the eyes of readers, who might have been skeptical that a woman could make a convincing private eye. Dalgliesh is present throughout the novel as Cordelia often recalls advice he gave to Bernie, who passed it on to her. Dalgliesh's advice will keep Cordelia from being caught by Dalgliesh himself later in the novel, and it is notable for more often reflecting a criminal mind than that of a police officer.

In addition to the subversion of gender roles and expectations, James explores the nature of relationships between parents and children. Cordelia's mother died when she was born, but from a "childhood of deprivation [Cordelia] evolved a philosophy of compensation" (25), creating an image of a mother who loves her and encourages her. Sir Ronald, on the other hand, appears initially sympathetic because of his desire to understand his son's suicide, but Sir Ronald murdered his son in a particularly depraved and violent fashion. Cordelia is not a blood relation to Bernie, but she knows he offered her partnership in the agency "not as a good conduct prize but an accolade of trust" (34). By contrast, Cordelia's actual father was an inconsistent and untrustworthy figure who thwarted her hopes for higher education by insisting she become his traveling secretary—not a good conduct prize at all.

Chapter 1 introduces key plot elements, beginning with the illegal gun Bernie bequeaths to Cordelia—this gun is what Miss Leaming will use to kill Sir Ronald. She also seeds traits and other clues that will later become relevant, including Sir Ronald's penchant for "absentmindedly" (41) and "apparently without thinking" (47) putting small objects into his pocket. Miss Leaming protests looking into Mark's motive for suicide by saying, "We knew nothing about him, nothing! So why wait until he's dead and then start finding out?" (44). This outburst seems odd until much later in the book, when we learn Miss Leaming was not only his mother but the one who found Mark hanged, dressed in women's underwear, and wearing lipstick. She cleaned and redressed his body to protect his reputation; Sir

Ronald's desire for an investigation threatens to reveal something about Mark she doesn't want anyone to know.

The "Bellinger bonus" is an example of foreshadowing. Sir Ronald came to the Pryde Agency on the recommendation of John Bellinger, who once hired detectives to track down the source of "an outbreak of obscene letters" (37). Bernie quickly discovered that the culprit was Bellinger's personal secretary, another clue to readers that appearances can be deceiving.

Chapter 1 also touches on a classic theme of detective fiction: the distinction between people who are honest and principled and those who appear that way but are deceitful and immoral. Bernie describes his suicide as "the easy way out" (16), and despite his status as an unsuccessful reject from the police force who barely scraped by, he emerges from the book as a man of principle. Sir Ronald, a man of statue and good repute, is revealed to be a truly heinous villain. Their deaths begin and end the novel. Bernie's is a true suicide and could be considered honorable; Sir Ronald's suicide is faked to cover up his criminal actions. James is interested in the many ways appearances can deceive and revisits this theme throughout the novel.

Chapter 2

Chapter 2 Summary

Cordelia begins her investigation into Mark Callender's suicide by interviewing his most recent employers at their estate, Summertrees: Major Markland; his wife, Mrs. Markland; and the Major's sister, Miss Markland. Cordelia is aware that her youthful appearance makes them skeptical about her qualifications but explains that as a result she might be "more successful [...] than the more usual type of private detective" (37). The Marklands ask why a private detective, not the police, and Cordelia explains that Sir Ronald isn't disputing the fact of Mark's suicide; he simply wants to understand the motivation for it, which "isn't really [the police's] kind of job" (37).

Cordelia learns that Mark responded to a help-wanted ad and must have realized the estate had a small, rustic cabin on the property before applying for the job. Major Markland admits he was surprised that a Cambridge student would want to become a gardener and live in a cabin without heat, hot water, or electricity, but he called Mark's former tutor, who confirmed that Mark had dropped out of school, not been asked to leave because of improper behavior or scandal. Major Markland claims that this information was all he needed; he did not see it his place to inquire further. The Marklands agree Mark was hard-working and kept to himself, though Miss Markland bitterly says, "He was a drop-out. He dropped out of university, apparently he dropped out of his family obligations, finally he dropped out of life. Literally" (57).

Miss Markland takes Cordelia to see the cabin where Mark lived and died. Cordelia is struck by the "little oasis of order and beauty [Mark had] created out of chaos and neglect" (61). Miss Markland tells Cordelia that her fiancé, with whom she spent a lot of time at the cottage, was killed in 1937, during the Spanish Civil War. She expresses strong emotions, saying:

> "I don't like your generation, Miss Gray. I don't like your arrogance, your selfishness, your violence, the curious selectivity of your compassion. You pay for nothing with your own coin, not even for your ideals. You denigrate and destroy and never build. You invite punishment like rebellious children, then scream when

you are punished. The men I knew, the men I was brought up with, were not like that" (65).

Cordelia is puzzled by Miss Markland's vehemence but interrogates her gently, learning that Miss Markland found Mark's body after he did not show up that morning to receive his assignment for the day. She discovered him barefoot wearing just a pair of workpants and describes the scene: a suicide note still in the typewriter, an unfinished cup of coffee on the table, and a pile of ashes in the fireplace, as if Mark had been burning a lot of papers before he killed himself.

Cordelia notices that Mark left a pitchfork stuck in the ground, just a few feet before he would have been finished turning over a row of earth. His gardening shoes were also casually discarded, and Cordelia thinks these things are at odds with Mark's otherwise obsessive neatness. Miss Markland tells her that a woman she presumed was Mark's girlfriend, whom she describes as foreign, probably French, and very rich, visited him the night before he died.

Cordelia is surprised when Miss Markland intuits that Cordelia plans to stay in the cabin but gives her permission, saying the other Marklands won't notice and wouldn't care if they did. Miss Markland leaves, and Cordelia examines first the outside and then the inside of the building, following the protocol Bernie drilled into her as received wisdom from Dalgliesh.

She determines that Mark was economical, tidy to the point of obsessive, and clean. She also discovers a crumpled-up page from a pornographic magazine in the yard; it is from the May edition, so it could have been there before Mark arrived. She finds several other oddities about the scene, including a cooked but untouched pan of stew and an open bottle of milk. She theorizes how Mark could have been obsessively tidy but killed himself with dinner on the stove. She wonders what to make of the visitor he had the night before his death. She discovers a blood donor's card in his wallet, showing his blood type is "B rhesus negative" (70), and is moved by the fact that "no one, neither the Marklands nor the boy's family or friends, had bothered to come back to clean up the pathetic leavings of his young life" (69). Despite her emotional reaction, Cordelia considers the facts and realizes that Mark may have been murdered.

Cordelia moves her things into the cottage, adding them to Mark's personal effects—her toothbrush next to his, her towel beside his own. She hides away the spoiled food as potential evidence and secrets her gun in a tree. Cordelia drives into Cambridge to continue her investigation. She follows a logical path, making an appointment to see the sergeant in charge of the case then hunting down and reading through the public record of the inquest. She plans to find and interview Hugo and Sophie Trilling later in the day.

Cordelia wanders around Cambridge and reflects on her youthful belief she would attend this famous university. She is moved by its beauty and walks about in a "trance of happiness" (78). Cordelia's itinerant revolutionary father first disregarded and then interrupted her education when he finally "discovered a need for his daughter;" she had to leave school at 16 to begin "her wandering life as a cook, nurse, messenger and general camp follower to Daddy and the comrades" (81). She thinks of a line from Blake: "Then saw I that there was a way to hell even from the gates of heaven" (82).

Cordelia leaves behind her wistful wanderings and goes to the police station, where she is surprised to learn that Sergeant Maskell was also put off by the incongruities at the scene of Mark's death. He shows her the leather strap and explains how unlikely it was that Mark could have formed the knot that killed him. Cordelia probes him repeatedly, and he agrees there are irregularities but says firmly, "it isn't what you suspect, it's what you can prove that counts" (87). The evidence he had simply didn't give him enough to point to a murder.

Cordelia asks if she can have the strap and the suicide note, and he agrees, saying, "no one else seems to want them" (87). When she sees the suicide note, Cordelia realizes two things are wrong about it. The first she keeps to herself, and the second is that it was typed by "an experienced typist" (88). Just as she is leaving the office, Maskell says to her:

> "There's one intriguing detail you may care to know. It looks as if he was with a woman some time during the day on which he died. The pathologist found the merest trace—a thin line only—of purple-red lipstick on his upper lip" (89).

Chapter 2 Analysis

Chapter 2 includes extensive and detailed descriptions of the scene of Mark's death and follows closely the detective's inner monologue as she considers the facts of the case. Cordelia's careful, rational approach to the evidence is contrasted by her emotional reactions to the scene, especially in how she moves into Mark's cottage, layering her belongings on top of his.

The other abrupt contrast of the chapter is between what Cordelia's life might have been and what it is. Learning that Cordelia hoped to attend Cambridge but was prevented from pursuing that dream by her selfish father gives her character more poignancy. James paints a rapturous picture of Cordelia's afternoon in Cambridge amid harmonious natural surroundings and glorious architecture, a place where "stone and stained glass, water and green lawns, trees and flowers were arranged in such ordered beauty for the service of learning" (82). Then, just moments later, she is holding the strap used in a murder and looking at a picture of Mark's corpse, the picture "uncompromising, unambiguous, a brutal surrealism in black and white" (85). This juxtaposition is another way James suggests Cordelia is out of place then subverts that suggestion when Cordelia interrogates the police officer and even notices something that will help her solve the case.

Though she was forced to leave school at 16, James presents Cordelia as well educated and erudite. She is keen enough to notice that Miss Leaming quoted Mark's supposed suicide note incorrectly, adding more words to it than were on the actual page. In allowing her to keep this knowledge to herself and from the reader, James is honoring the traditional trope of the detective having a superior intellect and setting up a surprising reveal for the reader. Without knowing what Cordelia does about the quotation, the reader could not possibly deduce that Miss Leaming was the one to find and clean Mark's body and leave the note. Given Miss Markland's odd behavior when she shows Cordelia the cottage, James offers her as a red herring, implying she may have had more to do with the scene. This unreliable narration is underscored by curious asides that don't seem to contribute to the plot. Miss Markland's story about her fiancé and the brief mention of "Carl […] in his Greek prison" (79) pique the reader's interest but ultimately have no real bearing on the story.

James's close third-person narration also blurs the lines between Cordelia's thoughts and the narrator's recitation of them, as in the capitalization of "Daddy" (81). It's possible to read "Daddy" as the narrator's sarcastic commentary or as Cordelia's own churlish conception—either way, "Daddy" implies a beloved endearment from a small child, but in context "Daddy" is a selfish, little-known figure who appears in the story only to crush his daughter's dreams.

Later, the narrator describes Cordelia deliberately choosing the persona she will use to "get information" from Sergeant Maskell, deciding to present an "unflirtatious competence […] to appear efficient, but not too efficient" (82), making clear her capacity to dissemble. What occasionally comes into question is how much dissembling the narrator is doing on Cordelia's behalf.

"Mark" can mean a dupe or a patsy, someone who has been targeted as the victim of a crime or a scam. James plays with this, echoing Mark's name in that of the Marklands, then going a step further to call the sergeant Maskell. Maskell is close to Markland, but instead of recalling a dupe, "mask" reminds us that things are not always what they seem, that appearances can be deceiving. This message is emphasized when Cordelia imagines hearing a "young masculine voice, unrecognized and yet mysteriously familiar," quoting William Blake, this time the famous line, "Then saw I that there was a way to hell even from the gates of heaven" (82). Blake's poetry is used to stress the themes of deception and disillusionment. James references Shakespeare's *King Lear* by naming her protagonist Cordelia and casting Sir Ronald as a Lear-like figure, driven in the end to madness.

Miss Markland again foreshadows trouble to come, saying to Cordelia, "It's unwise to become too personally involved with another human being. When that human being is dead, it can be dangerous as well as unwise" (66). In addition to giving Miss Markland an ominous aura, these lines remind the reader that the detective's job is inherently unnatural. Cordelia instead follows Dalgliesh's advice: "Get to know the dead person. Nothing about him is too trivial, too unimportant. Dead men can talk. They can lead you directly to their murderer" (45).

Chapter 3

Chapter 3 Summary

Cordelia finds Sophie and Hugo Trilling with Isabelle de Lasterie and Davie Stevens. They are startled when she explains why she is there, and Cordelia immediately becomes suspicious that they are hiding something. Hugo plays off their shock by saying they're surprised that Sir Ronald would hire a private investigator, as he "took no particular interest in his son when he was alive" (93). Cordelia learns that Mark's old nanny, Nanny Pilbeam, visited him at school on his 21st birthday, about six weeks ago.

Cordelia asks the friends to describe Mark. They are uncomfortable, and finally Hugo says abruptly, "He was sweet and he is dead. There you have it. [...] He was...a very private person. I suggest that you leave him his privacy" (96).

The four friends give Cordelia their alibi for the night of Mark's death, saying they were all at a play together, and urge Cordelia to leave the case alone. Cordelia tests Isabelle's knowledge of the play and Isabelle fails, not realizing that Cordelia has asked her opinion of a scene that does not exist in that text. Hugo defends Isabelle by saying she doesn't speak English well enough to understand the question. As they are leaving, Sophie invites Cordelia to her home, saying she would be glad to talk more about Mark.

Cordelia is certain the group is hiding something from her and wonders where any of them could have killed Mark. She ultimately doubts any of them are capable of having done so.

Cordelia goes to Sophie's house, where she learns that Sophie and Mark had been lovers for about a year. Sophie also tells Cordelia about Gary Webber, an "uncontrollable, violent" (104) autistic boy whom Mark befriended and came to babysit on occasion. Sophie and Mark had shared philosophical discussions about whether Gary and his family would be better off if Gary was dead. Sophie argued yes; Mark said no. Cordelia takes this moment to ask Sophie why she thinks Mark killed himself. Sophie refuses to discuss the topic then finally bursts out, "I didn't know him! I thought I did, but I didn't know the first thing about him!" (105). She also notes that meeting Miss Leaming at dinner one night felt like meeting a "prospective mother-in-law" (106).

The other friends arrive, and Cordelia eavesdrops on them. She overhears Isabelle asking the others if they can just pay her to stop her investigation. Hugo laughs and says, "not everyone can be bought" (106). Isabelle replies, "It is not, I think, a suitable job for a woman," and Cordelia remembers Bernie once telling her, "You can't do our job, partner, and be a gentleman" (107).

Cordelia goes punting with Sophie and Davie, getting a glimpse at what her afternoons might have been like if she went to Cambridge. The episode is carefully narrated with great attention to the scenery and the physical experience of the boat trip. Cordelia cannot bring herself to broach the topic of suicide in these circumstances, so she asks Davie about Sir Ronald. She learns that the lab he runs is very expensive and that Sir Ronald "cares a damn sight more" (110) for Chris Lunn than he did for his own son. Davie also reveals that Mark intended to return his inheritance to his father, and Cordelia realizes she must go to London and consult Mark's grandfather's will to find out who will benefit financially from Mark's death.

During the interlude on the boat, Cordelia's enthusiasm for the case begins to flag but she catches herself and resolves to see it through. The friends invite her to a party at Isabelle's house that night, and she goes in hopes of meeting Mark's former tutor, Edward Horsfall. While there, she discovers that Isabelle has a taste for fine art and a very decrepit, alcoholic chaperone.

Cordelia gets Isabelle alone and presses her about what happened when she last saw Mark. When Isabelle realizes Cordelia is referring to the visit she made to him the evening he died, she relaxes and speaks freely about Mark. She reveals that just before he dropped out of school, they took a trip to the seaside and along the way he stopped off to visit a doctor in a house, not an office. Cordelia presses for more information but Hugo interrupts, and Cordelia realizes they are trying to "shame her into giving up the case" (119).

Horsfall finally arrives at the party, and Cordelia asks him about Mark. When she suggests Mark may have been murdered, Horsfall says, "Unlikely, surely. By whom? For what reason? He was a negligible personality. He didn't even provoke a vague dislike except possibly from his father" (125). Horsfall then explains that Sir Ronald could not have killed Mark because, by coincidence, he and Sir Ronald were at a dinner together the night of Mark's death. Horsfall sat next to Sir Ronald and overheard him receive a telephone call from his son during the meal, around 8 p.m. Cordelia is surprised by this news, because Mark died between 7 and 9 p.m., so she tracks down the porter who took the call. The porter tells her he thought the caller was Mark, but when he next saw Sir Ronald after Mark's death, Sir Ronald told him the call had been from Chris Lunn, not Mark. Cordelia interrogates the porter, not believing that he was mistaken, but the porter insists that whoever Sir Ronald said the caller was is who the caller was.

Cordelia discusses the case with Hugo, who urges her to ask Chris Lunn about the call, describing Lunn as "absolutely sinister" (130). Cordelia despairs over her ability to solve the case alone, then realizes that being on her own is "no different from how essentially it had always been. Ironically, the realization brought her comfort and a return of hope" (131).

Cordelia returns to Mark's cottage and discovers someone took a large pillow and the strap she got from Sergeant Maskell and hung the pillow from the hook where Mark died, as if to resemble a dead body. Cordelia is terrified, as the perpetrator no doubt intended, but she notices that the knot used to hang the pillow is different from the one used on Mark.

Chapter 3 Analysis

Chapter 3 continues to contrast Cordelia's life and career as a private detective with the life she might have had if she had gone to school. Cambridge and its students are still described rapturously, as in Cordelia's memory of their excursion on the river: "a series of brief but intensely clear pictures, moments in which sight and sense fused and time seemed momentarily arrested while the sunlit image was impressed on her mind" (107).

When she attends the party at Isabelle's house, Cordelia resists the temptation to socialize for fun, instead concentrating on the case and treating the evening as part of her job. In an odd parody of a date, Hugo accompanies Cordelia to interview the porter. They leave in the middle of a party to conduct a murder investigation, hardly the usual reason a young man and young woman might step out. The theme of Cordelia's job being unsuitable for a woman comes up again, and Bernie's statement about how "you can't do our job and be a gentleman" is an example of James's enjoyment of irony. Cordelia can do the job exactly because she is not a gentleman; this work turns out to be uniquely suited to a woman.

While Cordelia is dogged in her investigation, she also has moments of despair when she doubts she will solve the case. However, though she doesn't realize it, her very doggedness is getting her closer and closer to the truth. Had she not persevered at the party until Horsfall arrived, she would not have heard him suggest Sir Ronald disliked his own son or learned that Sir Ronald received a phone call during dinner on the night Mark died. Later, she will realize that Sir Ronald had already killed his son then arranged for Chris Lunn to make the phone call. He had Lunn pretend to be Mark, to give him an alibi for Mark's death. However, once Sir Ronald learned someone interfered with Mark's body after Sir Ronald killed him, Sir Ronald realized that person could have done so prior to 8 p.m. Sir Ronald then changed his story and told the porter the call came from Lunn. Though the porter clearly suspected Sir Ronald was lying, he would not go against Sir Ronald's word.

When Cordelia discovers that Sir Ronald likely lied about the phone call, she cannot reconcile how he might have been involved in Mark's death with the fact that he hired her to investigate that death. When she eventually realizes he intended only for her to find out who faked Mark's suicide after Sir Ronald committed the murder, she is still confused as to why he wanted an investigation, given that there was some risk he would be found out. But Sir Ronald, with his fame and power, believes himself above the law and too smart to be outwitted by a private detective, especially a young woman like Cordelia. This hubris will be his downfall; as Davie points out to Cordelia, Sir Ronald "certainly knows how to pick his slaves" (110). In an ironic twist, Sir Ronald has picked Cordelia, who proves to be better at her job than he wanted her to be.

The way the four friends react to Cordelia's investigation makes her suspect their guilt; she does not yet know that they are trying to protect Mark's reputation. Only later will Isabelle reveal that she found Mark's body dressed in women's clothes and summoned Hugo, Sophie, and Davie to help clean him up. They intended to hide the evidence of what they believed was autoerotic asphyxiation gone wrong, believing incorrectly that their friend had a hidden side. Sophie tells Cordelia about Gary Webber because she wants to remember her friend and former lover for the good things he did, for the ways he was kind; she does not realize that Mark was murdered for being a principled person.

Mark had also told Sophie he intended to return his inheritance to his father. This is ironic because Sir Ronald kills him in part because he is afraid of what would happen if Mark refused the money. It's unclear whether Sir Ronald knew Mark intended to give him the money, or whether Sir Ronald still would have committed murder if he did. What

is clear is that Sir Ronald chose Chris Lunn over his own
son, trusting Lunn not to betray him but murdering Mark
out of fear that he might.

Chapter 4

Chapter 4 Summary

Cordelia continues her investigation, now tracking down
the florist who provided the wreath at Mark's funeral so she
can learn the identity of the woman she believes is Mark's
old nanny. At the florist's, Cordelia learns that "another
lady came to enquire from Sir Ronald Callender" (138) and
gets a name and address for Mrs. Goddard.

Cordelia and Mrs. Goddard have a conversation in the
graveyard where Mrs. Goddard has been tending her
husband's grave. Mrs. Goddard tells Cordelia that she had
been nanny to Mark's mother, Evelyn Bottley. She recounts
the family history, explaining that Evelyn's mother died
when Evelyn was born, and that Evelyn's father never
loved or respected her. Cordelia is sympathetic, seeing the
parallels to her own parents. Mrs. Goddard explains that
Evelyn met and married "Ronny Callender the Gardner's
son" (144). Cordelia is surprised to learn that Sir Ronald
grew up poor and realizes that Mark taking a job as a
gardener must have been a special slight for Sir Ronald,
reminding him of the poverty he worked so hard to escape.

Mrs. Goddard was sent away during Evelyn's pregnancy,
and she barely saw Evelyn after Mark was born because Sir
Ronald "couldn't bear anyone to be near her" (146), which
Mrs. Goddard sees as a sign of his devotion. But when she
was briefly alone with Evelyn, Evelyn gave Mrs. Goddard
a prayer book and asked her to promise to bring it to Mark
on his 21st birthday. Evelyn then said, "If you do [forget],

or if you die before then, or if he doesn't understand, it won't really matter. It will mean that God wants it that way" (146).

Mrs. Goddard brought the book to Mark and told no one else about it, not even Miss Leaming, who came to thank her for the wreath. Mrs. Goddard mentions that Mark asked her for the name of the doctor who treated his mother when she was dying. She also reveals that Miss Leaming had been an English teacher.

Cordelia believes the prayer book must contain a clue and races back to the cottage but cannot find any message in it. She continues to follow the trail of the investigation, tracking down the doctor who treated Evelyn. On the way to his house, she thinks someone in a van might be tailing her, possibly Chris Lunn, but manages to escape him. Once at the doctor's house she realizes he must be the same doctor Mark had stopped off to see on his way to the seaside with Isabelle. The doctor is extremely old and senile, but Cordelia gets confirmation that Mark had visited, as well as "a gentleman" who behaved pompously and spoke to the doctor "as if talking to a servant" (154). Mark, on the other hand, showed compassion for the elderly man, even offering to come visit him to give his wife a respite.

Cordelia returns to the prayer book, this time searching the page for St. Mark's Day. There she finds a "small pattern of hieroglyphics so faint that the mark on the paper was little more than a smudge" (156). Cordelia interprets the marks to be Evelyn's initials and the date she wrote the note, and that "AA" must stand for Evelyn's blood type. She remembers seeing Mark's blood donor card in his wallet and that he was group B.

Following this new clue, Cordelia devises a plan to discover Sir Ronald's blood type. She goes to Sophie's house to borrow the phone and eventually finds out that Sir Ronald is group A, and that "his son had to ring a month or so ago with the same enquiry" (158). Cordelia goes to the library to confirm her suspicion: "A man and wife both of whose bloods were A could not produce a B group child" (159).

Cordelia goes back to the cottage and catches Hugo and Isabelle sneaking in. They are there to reclaim the painting Isabelle had lent to Mark. Cordelia confronts them, saying, "There's something that both of you know and it would be better if you told me now" (164), otherwise she will involve Sir Ronald and possibly the police.

Hugo finally tells Cordelia the truth about the night of Mark's death, that Isabelle had not been at the play with them but had returned to the cottage to speak to Mark. Isabelle admits she "knew he was dead," adding, "it was horrible! He was dressed like a woman in a black bra and black lace panties […] he had painted his lips, all over his lips" (167). She describes seeing the pornographic images on the table, but when Cordelia asks her where the lipstick was, Isabelle can't remember seeing any lipstick. Cordelia realizes that if "she hadn't seen the lipstick, then it was because the lipstick hadn't been there to see" (169).

Hugo explains that Isabelle came to find him, and he and the rest decided to fake a suicide by cleaning Mark's body and dressing him in his own clothes. They "hadn't it in mind to fake a suicide note; that was a refinement somewhat outside our powers" (169). But when they returned to the cottage someone had been there before them and already cleaned and redressed the body. Hugo and Isabelle deny hanging the pillow in the cottage to try to scare her. Cordelia believes they are telling the truth and is more convinced than ever that Mark was murdered.

After Hugo and Isabelle leave, Cordelia decides to go to London to examine Mark's grandfather's will and see who would benefit financially from Mark's death. She then goes outside and finishes the digging Mark had abandoned. In preparation for her trip to London, she impulsively puts on Mark's belt: "The strength and heaviness of the leather so close to her skin was even obscurely comforting and reassuring, as if the belt were a talisman" (174).

Chapter 4 Analysis

The information Cordelia gets from Mrs. Goddard brings her closer to solving the case. She continues to pick up pieces of information because of her logical persistence. James makes extensive use of rhetorical questions throughout the novel, portraying Cordelia's thought process in minute detail, but no matter how many or what kind of theories she considers during these sessions, Cordelia still follows the evidence. Cordelia may speculate wildly, but she draws conclusions based on facts, echoing the words of Sergeant Maskell, who reminded her that it's what the evidence proves that matters.

The backstory Mrs. Goddard provides about Mark's parents is important to Cordelia's understanding of the case. However, it is even more important than the reader realizes because James, via her narrator, is withholding information from the reader. In Chapter 2, when Cordelia saw the supposed suicide note, she realized that Miss Leaming had quoted it incorrectly, but this fact was not revealed to the reader. Thus when Mrs. Goddard mentions that Miss Leaming was previously an English teacher, Cordelia knows what this signifies while the reader does not: Miss

Leaming could have written the suicide note since she likely knows Blake's work. Further, she wouldn't necessarily have needed to refer to the text when typing the note, which would cause her to misremember how much of it she had included. Cordelia and the narrator both prove to be unreliable, setting the reader up for a surprise reveal at the end of the story.

In a similar vein, when Cordelia tells Hugo and Isabelle that she thinks Mark was murdered, she immediately realizes she "shouldn't have revealed her suspicions" (168), and the reader is left to wonder why not. Hugo is described as undergoing a "subtle change of mood; was it irritation, fear, disappointment?" (168). This is a red herring: Hugo had nothing to do with Mark's murder, but James is casting him under a shadow of suspicion.

The visit with the old doctor is a reminder of Mark's sympathetic nature and of how cruel people can be to those they are supposed to love. Mrs. Gladwin, the doctor's husband, comes across as brutal and unforgiving in how she treats him, saying he "was glad enough to marry me when he wanted a nurse […] he was drinking all the practice profits away" (153). But Cordelia finds sympathy for her, seeing in Mrs. Gladwin "the hopeless rejection of help, the despair which no longer had energy even to look for relief" (154). These are qualities more often associated with the suicidal, and they are not qualities that Mark had, which gives Cordelia more confidence that he did not kill himself. His offer to sit with Dr. Gladwin is a reminder of his kindness to Gary Webber. While Cordelia had worried she was "becoming sentimentally obsessed with the dead boy" (68), by the end of Chapter 4 she thinks "it was impossible to believe that anything he had ever touched or owned could frighten or distress her" (174). This is more proof that Dalgliesh's admonition to get to know the dead is the right course of action, though it might seem unusual.

The belt is an important symbol in this chapter. Cordelia dons it as a protective token or talisman; this foreshadows that the belt will soon save her life. Her attention to detail, as in quizzing Isabelle about the lipstick, is also crucial to the plot's success. Early on Cordelia noticed that Sir Ronald had a habit of idly dropping small objects in his pocket; now she connects that habit to the lipstick and further develops a theory about Mark's death.

Hugo continues to be a foil for Cordelia: He is clever and smart but adopts a teasing, ironic tone—he is the aristocrat to Cordelia's determined plodder, a creature of refinement and elegance as Cordelia is a dog worrying a bone. In describing how he came to see his friend dead, he says, "A respectable, sensible, law-abiding citizen would have found the nearest telephone and rung the police. Luckily Isabelle is none of these things. Her instinct was to come to me" (169). His drollness is both a commentary on his social standing and a reflection of it. He lingers as a potential romantic partner for Cordelia, but his lack of gravity puts him at odds with her dedicated search for the truth.

Two new characters in this chapter bring two new names: Mrs. Goddard and the Gladwins. Mrs. Goddard's name contains allusions to godliness and to goodness, both of which align with her function in the plot. The Gladwins are in contrast: There is nothing "glad" or "winning" about their situation, which is another reminder that appearances can be deceiving.

The one difficulty of the novel arises in this chapter: the cryptic message Evelyn Bottley left for her son. It seems quite a leap for Mark or Cordelia to intuit that the "AA" under Evelyn's initials refers to her blood type. James's rich attention to detail and description allows her to camouflage important details in innocuous ways; Mark's wallet containing a blood donor card and both Mark and Cordelia realizing that Evelyn's coded message was about her blood type stand out as too obvious. The heavy-handedness of these elements contrasts with how James allows the narrator/Cordelia to conceal information from the reader, ultimately reminding us that in this genre, nothing can be trusted except the intellect and determination of the private eye.

Chapter 5

Chapter 5 Summary

Cordelia travels to London and tracks down a copy of Mark's grandfather's will. She discovers that there could be no financial motive for murder as "no one stood to gain by Mark's death except a long list of highly respectable charities" (177). After a quick visit to the office, which seems "even more sordid than when she had left it" (178), Cordelia returns to the cottage, where she is attacked just as she is putting the key in the door.

Her assailant covers her head with a blanket and drags her to an abandoned well on the property. He has removed the locked cover and now drops her in and replaces the heavy cap, leaving Cordelia treading water deep under the earth, in darkness.

Cordelia calms herself and realizes the well is narrow, just three feet in diameter. She devises a plan to brace her back against one side and her feet against the other to shimmy herself up. What follows is an agonizing struggle to make this climb. Eventually Cordelia gets to the top of the well and uses the strap she'd been wearing as a belt to harness herself in place. She cannot get the leverage needed to move the cover off the well and resolves to wait until someone passes by and she can yell for help. But then she realizes that whoever dropped her in the well surely intends for her death to look like an accident, which means they will have to return and make it look plausible that she could have pulled the cover off and fallen in. So, she waits "for death without hope and without further struggle" (184), until the cover begins to move.

The person removing the cover is Miss Markland, who was looking for Cordelia and happened to notice the well cover was out of place and the lock was smashed. Once Cordelia is safely in the cottage, she realizes she needs to get Miss Markland out of the way because the person who tried to kill her could return at any moment. She urges Miss Markland to go, saying, "I'm perfectly safe. Besides, I have a gun. I only want to be left in peace to rest" (186). But Miss Markland is moved by the experience of finding Cordelia left for dead in the well. She reveals that her four-year-old son, the child she had with her lover, fell to his death in that same well. Miss Markland is highly emotional in telling this story, and Cordelia grows upset; she finally shouts at the woman, "I don't want you here. For God's sake go!" (187). After Miss Markland leaves, Cordelia gets one of Mark's sweaters, which Miss Leaming knitted for him, gets her gun, and lays in wait for whoever tried to kill her.

Despite the physical toll of the day, Cordelia hides in the woods by the well, waiting, and eventually Chris Lunn arrives. He has her handbag, which she realizes he means to leave at the scene as further proof she fell in the well by accident. She jumps out to confront him, and he runs. Cordelia realizes she cannot shoot him, even though she has the gun, and so she chases him, first on foot and then in her car. He races away in his van, and she is behind him when he runs through an intersection and plows directly into a truck. His van is "crumpled under [the truck's] front wheel like a child's toy" (190), and then, as Cordelia is leaving the scene, the van explodes.

Cordelia goes into shock and pulls over onto the side of the road. As she is trying to calm herself, a man approaches; "she could smell the drink on his breath" (191). He accosts her until she threatens him with her gun. He leaves. Then, "her head fell forward and Cordelia slept" (192).

Chapter 5 Analysis

This brief chapter, just under 20 pages, takes us from staid government offices to an attempted murder, a thrilling car chase, and a violent death. James's pacing reflects the novel's sudden rush toward a conclusion as events pile up with increasing urgency. No longer is Cordelia gleaning information from casual conversation; now she is fighting for her life in a well. Miss Markland transforms from a slightly batty old lady to a tragic figure with a horrible death in her past. Chris Lunn goes from a menacing figure to an attempted murderer, then is incinerated by his own recklessness.

Two things in this chapter will come back to haunt Cordelia: She tells Miss Markland she has a gun, and she uses that same gun to deter a man who seems intent on assaulting her. Dalgliesh will find these witnesses, and they will make him suspicious of the story Cordelia concocts to explain Sir Ronald's death.

Another important object, the strap, saves Cordelia's life: It killed Mark, but it saved her. Similarly, the well killed Miss

Markland's son but returned Cordelia to the land of the living. All three of these objects—the gun, the strap, the well—have the potential to bring death or save life. James challenges the reader not to take anything at face value; she further pushes the point by insinuating that objects can be more than they seem. If Cordelia didn't have the gun, Lunn might not have run from her; thus an object associated with violence saves Cordelia's life.

This chapter also brings us back to Miss Markland and her unusual story. Early on we learned about her fiancé, with whom she spent time at the cottage, and who died before they could marry. Now we learn the couple had a son who also died, but none of this explains Miss Markland's hostility toward Cordelia and her generation. Miss Markland once told Cordelia that the cottage "holds certain embarrassing memories" (64) for her brother and sister-in-law. These memories are never fully explained, either. It's again unclear whether James intended them to have resolution or to remind us that no matter how much we learn or how much we know, we never get all the way to the end; we never get the entire truth.

Chapter 6

Chapter 6 Summary

Cordelia awakens in her car, somewhat recovered from the shock of her attempted murder and Chris Lunn's death. She drives directly to Sir Ronald's home. The front door is open, and Cordelia thinks "the house had waited for her" (194). As she is standing in the hall, Miss Leaming comes down the stairs and takes the pistol from her hand. She tells Cordelia Sir Ronald is in the study.

Cordelia confronts Sir Ronald with what she has figured out: He killed his own son and staged the scene to look like "an accidental death during sexual experiment" (196). Sir Ronald asks her who interfered with the body and staged the suicide; Cordelia responds, "I think I know, but I shan't tell you" (196). She accuses him of sending Chris Lunn to kill her. Sir Ronald insists he only asked Lunn to follow her, to ensure Sir Ronald was "getting value" for his investment in her services.

Sir Ronald denies all of Cordelia's accusations, and any evidence she might have used to prove the truth of them is gone. While Sir Ronald all but admits his guilt, he has plausible deniability, and she knows it. They get into an argument about the nature of good and evil, with Sir Ronald telling Cordelia that "Mark's death was necessary and, unlike most deaths, it served a purpose" (198). Cordelia is horrified that "a human being could be so evil," and Sir Ronald responds, "If you are capable of imagining it, then I'm capable of doing it" (199).

Cordelia tries to argue that Sir Ronald didn't need to kill Mark, but he is remorseless: "My son was a self-righteous prig. How could I put myself and my work in his hands?" (200). Cordelia threatens to reveal the murder, and Sir Ronald promises to ruin her if she does.

Miss Leaming comes into the room and shoots Sir Ronald dead with Cordelia's pistol, "an execution, neat, unhurried, ritually precise" (201). She says she did it because Mark was her son with Sir Ronald. Cordelia asks how she could be certain Sir Ronald was the murderer, and Miss Leaming reveals the lipstick used on Mark's face, which she had just found in the pocket of the suit Sir Ronald wore the night of Mark's death. Cordelia asks if Lunn could have planted the

lipstick, but Miss Leaming says no, because she and Lunn
were together in bed that night.

Cordelia devises a plan to cover up Sir Ronald's murder.
She walks Miss Leaming through the process of posing the
gun in Sir Ronald's hand, remembering a story Bernie told
her about a woman who nearly got away with killing her
husband except she had posed the body that made it clear
he could not have fired the shot himself. Cordelia uses this
knowledge to pose Sir Ronald in a way that makes suicide
seem plausible. The two women rehearse their stories for
the police then reveal their truths to each other. Miss
Leaming confesses that she was the one who found Mark,
cleaned his body, and faked the suicide note; Cordelia
explains how she came to suspect the woman. They call the
police and report the murder, using their cover story. The
cover story hinges on Sir Ronald having confiscated
Cordelia's gun at their first meeting and has the women
meeting in the hall and the hearing the shot.

While they wait for the police, Miss Leaming tells Cordelia
they will meet one last time after the inquest but should not
talk to each other until then. The women are nervous, but
then Cordelia says, "If we keep our heads this can't go
wrong" (209). Miss Leaming replies, "What is there to be
frightened of? We shall be dealing only with men" (209).

The police come and conduct their investigation. The
women stick to their story, and eventually the police send
them home. There is an inquest, which is a kind of trial to
determine the manner of a death. Miss Leaming and
Cordelia both testify. They lie, and the judge rules that Sir
Ronald committed suicide.

Outside the courtroom Cordelia meets Hugo, who is
dismissive of Sir Ronald's death, saying, "Death is the least

important thing about us" (222). He invites her to stay in Cambridge for a little while instead of returning to "town," but she refuses: "There was nothing in town for her, but with Hugo there would be nothing in Cambridge for her either" (223). She will stay until she has met with Miss Leaming, and then "the case of Mark Callender will be finished for good" (223).

Cordelia and Miss Leaming meet as they'd arranged—by "accident," at a church service. Miss Leaming wants to know if Cordelia will keep the agency going, and they discuss business for a moment, then Miss Leaming explains how they faked Evelyn's pregnancy and fooled everyone into thinking that Mark was really Evelyn's son. She explains why Nanny Pilbeam had to be sent away and how Sir Ronald would allow only that "incompetent fool Gladwin" (229) to attend Evelyn when she was ill. She even explains why Evelyn went along with the deceit: "she convinced herself that what we were doing was best for the child" (228). Miss Leaming notes that having a baby restored Evelyn to her father's good graces and his will.

Miss Leaming reveals that because she "wasn't allow to love" Mark, she "knit him endless jerseys" (230). She reflects on how he might have seen things: "Poor Mark, he must have thought that I was mad, this strange, discontented woman whom his father couldn't do without but wouldn't marry" (230).

Miss Leaming offers Cordelia a signed confession that would exonerate Cordelia if the investigation were ever reopened. Cordelia burns the note, saying, "Your lover shot himself. That is all that either of us need to remember now or ever" (231).

Cordelia returns to the cottage and prepares to leave, cleaning up and taking away her and Mark's things. On impulse she goes to the well and discovers that Miss Markland has planted flowers all around it. Cordelia is "torn between pity and revulsion" and leaves the cottage, convinced now the "case of Mark Callender was finished" (234).

Chapter 6 Analysis

This chapter finally reveals the whole story of Mark Callender's life and death. Typical of the genre is the confrontation Cordelia has with Sir Ronald, in which she lays forth her accusations and he parries them while gloating that he is going to get away with the crime. He explains how carefully and cleverly he planned it, and since what little evidence she had is gone, it seems likely that Sir Ronald will win this round. But justice is served by Miss Leaming, who avenges her son's death by killing her lover, his father. Cordelia has conversations with Sir Ronald and Miss Leaming about the nature of love and a parent's responsibilities to a child, bringing to a close two important themes of the novel. Sir Ronald is revealed to be truly evil, but Cordelia's determination to cover up his death shows the strained fine line the detective walks in her pursuit of truth and justice. Sir Ronald committed a mortal sin, but Cordelia conspires to keep his murder a secret, thus denying Mark's murderer justice.

Cordelia's inspiration to disguise Sir Ronald's death as a suicide has roots in the way Sir Ronald staged Mark's death, but it also recalls Bernie Pryde's death. At the beginning of the novel Bernie died an unambiguous suicide, with a clear reason left behind for his actions; by the end there are no more neat and tidy plot lines, just a seething mess of lies, deceit, and betrayal.

James displays some delight in having Cordelia and Miss Leaming get away with murder. The trope of the brilliant detective who outsmarts everyone else is given a little zing by having that brilliant detective be a woman who outsmarts a bunch of men.

Miss Leaming and Cordelia's last meeting serves as the denouement of the novel, with Miss Leaming answering any remaining questions the reader might have about how events unfolded. It's typical of the genre to ensure all loose ends are wrapped up and tucked away, and Miss Leaming does a fine job of it. The chapter's final scene, in which Cordelia discovers that Miss Markland has turned the well into a kind of shrine, reminds us that objects are imbued with meanings by the people who regard them.

Chapter 7

Chapter 7 Summary

Cordelia returns to her office and discovers a check for her expenses has come from Sir Ronald's estate. She is contemplating what her future might hold when the telephone rings and she is summoned to meet with Chief Superintendent Dalgliesh. The novel then skips forward, picking up 10 days later, when Cordelia is on her third visit to Dalgliesh.

The narrator recaps how the prior visits went, what Dalgliesh has been like, and how Cordelia has stuck to her story about Sir Ronald's death. Dalgliesh clearly suspects her of not telling the full truth. He surprises her with deep knowledge of her investigation, having clearly traced her path. He horrifies her by accusing her of lying about Sir Ronald confiscating the gun. He has testimony from Miss Markland and the drunken stranger who accosted her, both of whom told Dalgliesh she claimed to have a gun during the time it was supposedly in Sir Ronald's possession.

Cordelia is on the verge of confessing everything when they are interrupted by a message that announces Miss Leaming has died in a car accident. Dalgliesh tells Cordelia she can go—"there's not much point in you staying" (246)—implying he has worked out that Miss Leaming killed Sir Ronald. Cordelia breaks down into "dramatic and uncontrollable crying" (247), behavior completely at odds with the calm cool she has demonstrated through the novel.

In her anger and grief, Cordelia lashes out at Dalgliesh for not coming to Bernie's funeral. Dalgliesh is surprised to realize that Bernie was her partner and admits "this case might have ended rather differently if I [had]" (247). Cordelia is pleased by this admission of respect.

Dalgliesh goes to report to his superior officer and explains all he has seen and heard. The assistant commissioner points out there's no way to prove these assertions, and Dalgliesh agrees. He speaks of Bernie with grudging admiration: "He wasn't unintelligent, not totally without judgement, but everything, including ideas, came apart in his hands" (248). They agree not to pursue the inquiry further. Dalgliesh regrets not finding out what happened to Bernie but says, "I find it ironic and oddly satisfying that Pryde took his revenge" (230).

The novel concludes with Cordelia returning to her office to find a prospective client waiting on her doorstep.

Chapter 7 Analysis

The novel's main conflict was addressed and resolved in Chapter 6. James surprises the reader by tacking on a final chapter in which she finally brings her more famous character, Dalgliesh, face-to-face with Cordelia. The chapter functions as a showdown, a battle of the wits, and though Cordelia prevails, Dalgliesh knows they both know the truth of what happened in Sir Ronald's study. The problem is that Dalgliesh can't prove it, and when Miss Leaming, Sir Ronald's murderer, dies, Dalgliesh must admit there is no further reason to pursue the case.

The novel comes full circle in this chapter, with Dalgliesh realizing that it was his old comrade, Bernie Pryde, who trained up the young woman who is allowing someone to get away with murder. Dalgliesh takes a kind of perverse pride in this realization, underscoring the fine line that separates criminals from those who catch them.

Cordelia's breakdown is her first real loss of control in the novel, and it comes just as she realizes she is getting away with her plan. Cordelia's tears are unusual for a private detective, but James allows her to shed them, confronting the reader's expectations that a successful detective must be a hardened, embittered man.

The client Cordelia finds on her doorstep hopes to discover whether his "lady friend […] is getting a bit on the side" (250), exactly the kind of job one might find unsuitable for a woman. This is James's last winking acknowledgment that Cordelia both exemplifies and defies the tropes of the genre.

Cordelia Gray

At 22, Cordelia becomes the sole proprietor of a failing detective agency after her partner's suicide. She was trained as a secretary but has a keen intellect and an instinct for asking questions when events don't make sense. Cordelia was orphaned by the death of her father, with whom she had been traveling as a secretary. Her mother died at Cordelia's birth; Cordelia's relationship with her parents is paralleled in other parent-child relationships of the novel.

Cordelia has many of the characteristics of the traditional private detective: She is dogged, she follows her own moral code, and she uses logic and reason to follow clues where they lead, without letting emotion interfere. But because she is young and a woman, she also subverts many of the expectations of this archetype. This would have been unusual and surprising at the time the novel was written, in the 1970s.

Cordelia is a hero and an antihero: She solves the case of Mark's murder but prevents his murderer from being arrested or tried in court, essentially invoking her own justice for him. She is a conundrum: well educated though she was forced to leave school early, and capable of poetic thoughts but a realist. Because Cordelia is a woman in what is traditionally a man's role, she provides a new spin on an old, established character type and holds up a mirror to the assumptions and stereotypes typical of the time.

Cordelia's name comes most recognizably from *King Lear* and signals James's interest in how names can hint at a character's destiny. Sir Ronald functions most closely as the Lear figure, asking Cordelia for help, sending her away on a mission, and then revealing his madness and dying in front of her.

Cordelia's final confrontation with Adam Dalgliesh establishes her as his equal or perhaps even his better, fully representing that a woman is just as capable—if not more so—than James's more famous detective.

Mark Callender

Mark is only a corpse and a memory. His death is the novel's central mystery, and the revelation that he was killed by his own father furthers the novel's consideration of the conflicts between good and evil, children and parents, and virtue and greed.

Mark is presented as something of an enigma. Like other symbolic objects in the novel, Mark is whoever other people perceive him to be. Cordelia discovers the true story of his life and death in bits and pieces; along the way she is presented with interpretations of his personality and actions that reflect more on the person making the observation than on Mark himself.

Cordelia solves Mark's murder by getting to know him. The clues he leaves behind allow her to discover his murder was not a suicide or a sexual experimentation gone wrong but a cold-blooded sacrifice to his father's greed. Mark is a martyr to principle, and it is his own goodness and morality that gets him dead.

Bernie Pryde

Bernie Pryde is a former police officer who opened a detective agency. He hires Cordelia first as a secretary and then promotes her to partner before he commits suicide after a diagnosis of cancer. Bernie never appears in the novel except as a corpse and in Cordelia's memories. He is a pathetic character who was fired from the police and unsuccessful as a detective, and who left Cordelia nearly broke and basically homeless. But he is also a sympathetic character; he is a kind and generous surrogate father to Cordelia, and he trains her so well she succeeds without him.

Bernie's last name asserts that despite his failings he was a man of principle and pride. He attributed much of the wisdom he passed on to Cordelia to his former supervisor Dalgliesh, but it's possible some of that wisdom came from Bernie directly and he obscured that out of pride. Two of the novel's key themes are that appearances can be deceptive and that there are two sides to everything. Bernie's pride forced him to commit suicide (because he's "seen what the treatment does to people and I'm not having any" [16]); it also gave him a reason to live after Dalgliesh took away the only job he ever wanted.

Sir Ronald Callender

Sir Ronald is a semi-famous microbiologist who runs a large laboratory out of his own home. He has one son, Mark, and a secretary/mistress, Miss Leaming. He also employs Chris Lunn as a laboratory assistant/general aide. He hires Cordelia to investigate his son's death on the pretense of discovering why Mark committed suicide. His real aim is to find out who interfered with Mark's body after Sir Ronald killed him.

Sir Ronald has two sides: He murdered his own son but is an excellent father figure to Chris Lunn. Sir Ronald's psychical appearance mirrors his transition from a respected and prosperous scientist to a madman murdered by the mother of his only child. A central question around Sir Ronald is why he hires a private detective to investigate his son's death. Presumably he believed he was too clever to be caught by that investigation. He underestimates Cordelia, and she outwits his efforts to remove her from the case and uncovers his deceptions.

Sir Ronald is a peer of the realm, an exalted position, who worked his way up from humble beginnings. He is also a liar, a manipulator, a cheater, a bully, and a murderer. James uses these juxtapositions to underscore her theme that things are not always what they seem.

Miss Elizabeth Leaming

Elizabeth Leaming is Sir Ronald's secretary/mistress and the unacknowledged mother of his only child. She is also his murderer. A complex figure, she is complicit in deceiving Mark about his parentage but cared for him deeply from afar. The suicide note she writes for him quotes William Blake and reflects her own liminal status— neither in heaven nor in hell but hung in an empty space somewhere in between.

Miss Leaming presents as mysterious and secretive; she is a cool and efficient secretary but appears at the end of the novel in a "long red dressing gown" (194)—red, the color of sex, blood, death, and hell. Miss Leaming murders Sir Ronald, acting as an agent of divine justice or retribution, and then offers her signed confession to Cordelia, signaling her willingness to be judged for her actions. As a mother, she fails and then avenges her son, reflecting the dual nature of parentage that recurs as a theme throughout the novel.

Adam Dalgliesh

Dalgleish is a chief superintendent with New Scotland Yard, home of the Metropolitan Police. He is Bernie Pryde's former superior and P.D. James's most famous protagonist. He is heard but not seen until the last chapter. His presence gives this book authority while his absence allows Cordelia to step into the spotlight. Dalgliesh, like Cordelia, exists in a realm of moral ambiguity, which is the hallmark of the detective's code. He is a police officer but thinks like a criminal. He knows that Cordelia is lying to him but allows her to get away with hiding the identity of a murderer. He is a loner, beholden only to his own moral code. He is careful, thorough, and brilliant, and when Cordelia beats (or ties) him at his own game, that victory cements her status as his equal—or perhaps even his better.

Chris Lunn

Chris Lunn is an orphan Sir Ronald brought into his household as a teenager. Sir Ronald is closer to Lunn than to his own son, though he trains Lunn as an assistant rather than encouraging him to be a scientist in his own right. Davie describes Lunn as Sir Ronald's "slave" (110). Lunn makes a phone call that could provide Sir Ronald with an alibi and tracks and harasses Cordelia on Sir Ronald's instruction; he is killed when she pursues him and he crashes his van. Lunn is a foil to Mark Callender, the evil son to Mark's angelic one.

Evolving the Role of the Private Eye

In detective fiction a key theme is usually how the detective
is a part of but apart from society. Characteristic traits
include being a loner, adhering to a personal moral code,
and using their superior intellect to solve the case. When
James was writing and publishing this novel, in the early
1970s, the women's liberation movement was still in its
early stages in America and was little known in Britain. In
making her protagonist a woman, James was challenging
cultural norms; because she was writing so-called genre
fiction, it was less of a transgression than other feminist
statements, but it should still be considered in the context
of the time and of James's own struggles to write and
publish as a woman in a traditionally male-dominated
genre.

Tellingly, Cordelia's youth and sex are the main ways in
which she varies from the standard portrayal of the private
eye. She is a bit of a romantic and indulges in theorizing
via rhetorical questions, but that behavior is within the
boundaries of the traditional role. In every other way, she
functions as a private detective should: She is an outsider
and a loner; she has few assets beyond her wits; she has a
keen intellect; she doggedly pursues the clues she finds; she
makes a leap of intellect that allows her to solve the case.
She also adheres to her own moral code, which doesn't
exactly match up with that of the police, as she helps Miss
Leaming get away with murder.

James introduced Cordelia after four successful novels
featuring Adam Dalgliesh, who is a member of the police
force but also functions more like a private detective than
an officer of the law. In bringing Cordelia into his universe,

James was broadening the range of her work, though still writing within the confines of the genre. Cordelia is an appropriate foil to Dalgliesh, as she is like him and unlike him at the same time. In ensuring that Dalgliesh's presence in the novel legitimizes Cordelia, and in fitting her so neatly into the genre's stereotypes, James pushed the envelope: Cordelia may be a woman, but she functions just as a man would. Her final confrontation with Dalgliesh cements this status: She beats him at his own game, and he acknowledges this with a kind of delighted pride. Rather than reinvent the genre with a new breed of private detective, James expanded the types of characters who can credibly populate it.

Money as the Root of Evil

The private detective must follow a specific and unyielding moral code. These codes often include stipulations about money, which usually represents evil or corruption. In this novel money is an important theme: Sir Ronald kills for it, Mark dies for it, and Cordelia won't take it and can't be bought by it.

Rich characters are often portrayed as dissolute; their unencumbered wealth giving them license to behave however they see fit. Sir Ronald is a classic example: He grows up poor, working with his father as a gardener. He marries the daughter of the man who owns those gardens and, through a combination of her fortune and his own hard work, becomes a wealthy and respected scientist. But the money is never enough for him, and he does terrible things to ensure or obtain it. He has an affair with his secretary then convinces her and his wife to pass the baby off as Evelyn's instead of Miss Leaming's, to ensure Evelyn's father's estate will go to Evelyn and the boy, Mark. When Sir Ronald realizes that Mark's discovery of this secret might expose him and cost him that fortune, Sir Ronald reacts out of fear and kills his own son. He convinces himself he had to kill Mark because he couldn't risk the groundbreaking science being done in his lab, but he ultimately kills Mark for money.

In contrast to Sir Ronald, Mark grew up in privilege, free from want or worry thanks to the safety net of his mother's fortune. He was studying at Cambridge University when he discovered his father's secret. His mother hoped he would find out after his 21st birthday, presumably so that he would be old enough to decide what to do with the knowledge. Mark, being a young man of principle, decided to reject the money due to him when he turned 25 because he believed it was coming to him through trickery and deception. Consciously or not, he took the reverse of the path his father did, giving up his comfortable lifestyle to work as a gardener, for a pittance. This decision is partly why Sir Ronald does not trust his son not to expose him; Sir Ronald cannot imagine that someone who would choose the humble lifestyle he fought so hard to escape could be trusted to keep such a damning secret. He calls Mark a "self-righteous prig" (200), fully expecting his son to ruin his reputation.

Isabelle, another wealthy character, is less corrupted by her wealth than Sir Ronald but is still the least intelligent, least studious of Mark's four friends. However, her passion for art redeems her in Cordelia's eyes. Her chaperone, on the other hand, over-indulges in alcohol, and James paints an unsparing portrait of her as louche and disgusting. Isabelle wants to pay Cordelia to leave the case alone, prompting Sophie to say Cordelia "can't" be bough. Her resistant to temptation, to corruption, is a defining feature of the private detective, and Cordelia fills the role well. She ends up taking nothing but expenses from Miss Leaming, refusing to profit from the case despite the amount of time and personal risk she assumed. Again, Cordelia's adherence to her moral code is noble, even if it leaves her back where she started: penniless and alone.

The Value of a Life

Morality is another key theme of the novel, especially around who lives and who dies. Two murderers go unpunished in this book, at least unpunished by the criminal justice system. Mark's justice comes when his biological mother murderers his father in retribution for his death; Sir Ronald's justice comes when Miss Leaming is killed in a car accident just a few weeks after murdering him. The narrative's moral arc promises that no one gets away with murder, at least not for long, but it does not require the court system to decide that.

There are many deaths in this book: It opens with Bernie's suicide, then Mark is killed, then Chris Lunn, then finally Sir Ronald and Miss Leaming. Other characters grieve losses—Cordelia has just lost her father and, long ago, her mother. Sir Ronald lost his wife, and Mark his purported mother. Miss Markland lost a finance and a young son. If some of these deaths make sense—Bernie's because he won't face the indignity of cancer treatment, Sir Ronald's because he murdered his son—others do not. Chris Lunn tried to murder Cordelia but failed, yet he dies in return. Miss Markland's fiancé died in a war, which might be expected; her small child's death by drowning in the well is not.

Death often represents punishment, and it is interesting to consider who "earns" their death and who is punished by another's death. In the case of Miss Markland, the death of her child could be considered punishment for having him out of wedlock, a harsh and perhaps unfair outcome. Sir Ronald is punished for killing Mark with his own death; Miss Leaming's death is less well earned. In the world of the detective novel, punishment can be harsh, and no one knows that better than the detective herself, especially as she is the only person left alive with that knowledge. (Dalgliesh knows, too, but cannot reveal that knowledge lest he face culpability from his superiors for being complicit in the cover up of a crime.)

Because Cordelia does not reveal her knowledge to Dalgliesh, though she is tempted, she makes herself the arbiter of justice, the person who decides when a crime has been committed. While Miss Leaming could not face a trial for Sir Ronald's murder, knowing the whole truth of Mark's life and death might have made a difference to his friends, even to his old nanny. In making the decision not to reveal this information, Cordelia sets herself up as the ultimate authority in matters of good and evil, right and wrong. She may be young and a woman, but she demonstrates the moral fortitude that is the hallmark of the private eye.

The Elusive Nature of Truth

A detective is, by definition, in pursuit of truth. Whether working for the police or as a private citizen, a detective sets out to discover exactly what happened. Along the way, the detective will encounter lies, misrepresentations, and deceit. She must sort through these to find out what is real, relying on facts and evidence to guide her. As Sergeant Maskell says, "it isn't what you suspect, it's what you can prove that counts" (87).

However, another theme of the detective novel genre is unreliable narration. Because this book is written in the close third person, it's difficult to tell which thoughts belong to Cordelia and which come from the narrator. Cordelia deliberately withholds information from the reader, information that would allow the reader to suspect Miss Leaming's role in Mark's death. Because James lets us see Cordelia keep that secret, it leads the reader to wonder what other secrets Cordelia might be keeping. In this way, the only person who ever knows the entire truth is the detective; the rest of us are invited in as she sees fit.

The irony of the detective's search for truth is that truth can be subjective; it can be what we want it to be. Cordelia may know that Sir Ronald killed his son, but she cannot truly know whether he did it for the good of science, as he claimed, or because he did not love his son and did not want him in the way of his own plans and ambitions. While the distinction may be slight, the difference is a more noble motive versus a less noble one. Neither is a good excuse for murder, but one is borne of delusion and the other of evil.

Several characters protest the search for truth, each for their own reasons. Miss Leaming, Sophie, Hugo, Davie, and Isabelle fear an investigation into Mark's death because they all believe they are protecting his reputation from whatever scandal might ensue should anyone else discover the way they found his body—dressed in women's underwear, surrounded by pornographic images. Cordelia protests Dalgliesh's search for truth because she does not want to see Miss Leaming punished for Sir Ronald's murder. Once Miss Leaming is dead, she keeps him away from the truth, now to protect her own reputation and Bernie's memory.

There is a proverb that says "the truth will set you free." In detective fiction the opposite is usually the case: Knowing the truth of a crime puts a person at risk of becoming a victim or a criminal. Miss Leaming and Cordelia become both victims and criminals; their success in doing so is a commentary on how the men of the novel fail to suspect them and on their willingness to engage in thoughts and actions considered unsuitable for women. In displaying behavior typical of men, they get away with murder.

Mark's Strap/Belt

The strap Mark Callender was hanged with is the most important symbol in this text. The knot tied into the strap confirms that Mark was murdered, as he could not have created that knot himself. The different knot used to hang the pillow tells Cordelia that it is not the murderer who is trying to scare her. The belt is also a "talisman" for Cordelia, and it saves her life when she is trapped in the well. The belt further symbolizes the theme of duality: It can bring death and give life.

Deceptive Appearances

Throughout the novel what is outside is contrasted against what is inside. Sir Ronald is a respected scientist and peer; he is also a murderer. Cordelia is a pretty young woman; she is also a ruthlessly intelligent and resourceful detective. Bernie was a hack; he also trained Cordelia to be an even match for Dalgliesh. Isabelle is vapidly beautiful; she also has a keen eye for fine art. Amid these contradictions Mark exists as an enigma, revealed only through the way others describe him, which suggests that appearances are reality.

Exteriors Reflecting Interiors

The symbolic importance of a house's exterior is a motif used throughout the novel to underscore James's theme that appearances can be—but aren't always—deceiving. The Callender house is "as artificial and unsubstantial as a film set [....] a heavy silence lay over it and the rows of elegantly proportioned windows were empty eyes" (38). Summertrees, the Markland estate, is "an intimidatingly ugly house" (54), while the cottage Mark occupied had a "gentle melancholy charm" (61). Sophie Trilling's house has the same layout as one Cordelia lived in as a foster child, but Sophie's house has a "clean, sun-scented interior," while Cordelia's unhappy memories include "the strong odor of unwashed napkins, cabbage and grease" (100). Later, after Cordelia is stymied in her pursuits, the windows of Sophie's home appear "as blank as dead rejecting eyes" (131).

Bernie's Gun

Like Mark's strap, Bernie's gun has a dual nature. It represents a threat of violence when Cordelia uses it to scare off Chris Lunn, thus saving her life and leading to his death. Cordelia looks to the gun as protection, but it nearly causes her downfall when Dalgliesh discovers that she has lied about its whereabouts. Guns, like the strap, can reveal the truth of a murder versus a suicide—but Cordelia wields the gun carefully enough that it cannot give away Sir Ronald's murder.

Gary Webber

Gary Webber, the autistic boy who takes a liking to Mark, is a foil for Mark's relationship with Sir Ronald. Sir Ronald kills his son out of fear that Mark will expose him as a cheat and a liar. Sophie Trilling argues that a boy like Gary is better off dead, as he is such a drain on his family and society. Mark, a principled and well-regarded young man, is the opposite, a credit to society and his family. While Gary lives, Mark dies. At the end of the novel, Cordelia confronts Sir Ronald, saying Mark's death would matter to Gary, but Sir Ronald does not know who Gary Webber is, a further reminder that Sir Ronald did not know his son at all.

1. "It isn't a suitable job for a woman." (Chapter 1, Page 25)

    This is the first—but not last—mention of how Cordelia's gender makes her ill-suited for her role. This is a repeated theme throughout the novel. Here the lines are especially ironic, as they are said by a female bartender, another role that could be considered unsuitable for a woman.

2. "She had quickly learned that to show unhappiness was to risk the loss of love. Compared with this early discipline of concealment, all subsequent deceits had been easy." (Chapter 1, Page 26)

    These lines establish Cordelia's suitability for being a private investigator: She was brought up in foster homes where she learned to lie, cementing her status as an outsider and an unreliable narrator.

3. "Bernie had needed to be a detective as other men needed to paint, write, drink or fornicate." (Chapter 1, Page 30)

    Cordelia is reflecting on Bernie's dismissal from the police. The reason for that is never given, but she assumes it must be unfair because the job was his calling. This is the nearest James gets to salty, base language, used here to show the seriousness of the statement. As the reader realizes Cordelia has the same calling, this line helps us understand why she isn't jealous of Sophie's life, or Isabelle's, and how she engages with her work, no matter unsuitable it may seem: She doesn't feel she has a choice.

4. "This lust always to know! It's only prying. If he'd wanted us to know, he'd have told us." (Chapter 1, Page 42)

Miss Leaming says this while Sir Ronald is explaining his desire to understand Mark's death. Miss Leaming is hoping to hide what she believes is Mark's sexual experimentation; the word "lust" is a clue to her area of concern.

5. "I'm not prepared to go on in this uncertainty. My son is dead. *My* son. If I am in some way responsible, I prefer to know." (Chapter 1, Page 42)

In these lines, addressed to Cordelia at their initial interview, Sir Ronald emphasizes "my son," though his son's biological mother is also in the room. Sir Ronald knows that he was responsible for Mark's death—he killed the boy—so it's strange that he suggests he may be responsible.

6. "Get to know the dead person. Nothing about him is too trivial, too unimportant. Dead men can talk. They can lead you directly to their murderer." (Chapter 1, Page 45)

Cordelia remembers this wisdom from Dalgliesh. Though she does not yet know Mark has been murdered, she follows Dalgliesh's advice and it works.

7. "It's unwise to become too personally involved with another human being. When that human being is dead, it can be dangerous as well as unwise." (Chapter 2, Page 66)

Miss Markland says this to Cordelia after letting her into Mark's cottage. Miss Markland may be alluding to her own dead fiancé in the first sentence; in the second, she sounds like she's giving an ominous warning, but it's more likely she is remembering her own dead son. Miss Markland is repeatedly dangled as a potential bad actor, but she is a red herring each time.

8. "She saw the picture as a contrast between the worlds of the intellect and action and tried to remember where she had seen similar paintings. The comrades—as Cordelia always thought of that ubiquitous band of fellow-revolutionaries who attached themselves to her father—had been very fond of exchanging messages in art galleries and Cordelia had spent hours walking slowly from picture to picture, waiting for the casual visitor to pause beside her and whisper his few words of warning or information." (Chapter 2, Page 71)

Cordelia is looking at a painting in Mark's cottage. In this aside the narrator gives us a glimpse into Cordelia's unusual upbringing. She must have served as a go-between for her father and his comrades, and in this way she became educated about art. There are few references to Cordelia's father and his politics, but those included are intriguing in their mystery.

9. "It was only in fiction that the people one wanted to interview were sitting ready at or in their office, with time, energy and interest to spare." (Chapter 2, Page 77)

Cordelia is reflecting on having to wait a few hours before getting an appointment to see Sergeant Maskell. James is playing heavily with irony as, of course, Cordelia is a fictional character in a work of fiction.

This sly wink at the reader is a hallmark of James's playful sense of humor.

10. "Cordelia had stayed on at the Convent for the six most settled and happy years of her life, insulated by order and ceremony from the mess and muddle of life outside." (Chapter 2, Page 80)

   Cordelia's father took a haphazard interest in her upbringing, and when he did not answer a letter from the content where she had accidentally been sent for schooling, she stayed there for six years. The ironic contrast between her happiest times in an orderly place and the mess and muddle she exists in as a private detective underscores the deep sadness Cordelia feels about having the life she'd hoped for taken away from her.

11. "You can't do our job, partner, and be a gentleman." (Chapter 3, Page 107)

   Cordelia is guiltily eavesdropping on Sophie, Davie, Hugo, and Isabelle when she remembers these words of wisdom from Bernie. The irony is that Cordelia is not and could never be a gentleman, which is another way James demonstrates how well suited she is to the job.

12. "She was in danger of being lulled into a gentle acceptance of defeat; viewing all her suspicions as a neurotic hankering after drama and notoriety, a need to justify her fee to Sir Ronald. She believed that Mark Callender had been murdered because she wanted to believe it. She had identified with him, with his solitariness, his self-sufficiency, his alienation from his father, his lonely childhood. She had even—most

dangerous presumption of all—come to see herself as his avenger." (Chapter 3, Page 108)

Cordelia has a moment of self-doubt while out punting with Mark's friends. They are trying to distract her from the case, and it's working; it's unclear whether the lines above are Cordelia's thoughts or the narrator's observation. Ironically, while Cordelia isn't officially Mark's avenger, she does discover the truth of his murder and allow his mother to avenge him.

13. "In that moment Cordelia knew how close she had come to giving up the case. She had been suborned by the beauty of the day, by sunshine, indolence, the promise of comradeship, even friendship, into forgetting why she was here. The realization horrified her." (Chapter 3, Page 112)

In her time punting on the river, Cordelia finds herself enjoying the moment and the experiences that she might have taken for granted had she ended up at Cambridge. But the private detective's code requires that person to remain an outsider, to shun beauty, indolence, and friendship. James stresses Cordelia's horror to firmly show that she is choosing her life, not accepting it as a substitute.

14. "She was insensible with drink. She lay there emitting puffs of foul, whisky-laden breath which rose like invisible balls of smoke from the half-open mouth [...] Her thin lips were thickly painted, the strong purple stain had seeped into the cracks around the mouth so that the body looked parched in an extremity of cold. Her hands, the gnarled fingers brown with nicotine and laden with rings, lay quietly on the counterpane. Two of

the talon-like nails were broken and the brick-red polish on the others was cracked or peeled away." (Chapter 3, Pages 114-15)

James has a keen eye for description, and Mademoiselle de Congé gets a thorough treatment. De Congé is derelict in her duties as Isabelle's chaperone, and James makes sure that her failure is reflected in her grotesque and debauched condition. It's an interesting amount of time and effort to spend on an inconsequential character, but de Congé's example suggests that enjoying parties like the one Cordelia is attending leads to dissolution and decay.

15. "[A]lienated by the last six years from her own generation, [Cordelia] found herself intimidated by the noise, the underlying ruthlessness and the half-understood conventions of these tribal matings." (Chapter 3, Page 121)

Cordelia is at Isabelle's party, and James uses the opportunity to again show how Cordelia is not a part of her peer group, no matter how much she looks the part. James ensures that the reader senses Cordelia's disdain for those peers, rather than allowing us to assume she is jealous or wishes to be part of them.

16. "Mark said that he chose history because we have no chance of understanding the present without understanding the past [...] Actually, of course, the reverse is true; we interpret the past through our knowledge of the present." (Chapter 3, Page 125)

Mark's former tutor says this to Cordelia, but Horsfall's statement doesn't ring true based on our knowledge of the present. Mark's death was caused by his investigation into the past, which allowed him to understand the present.

17. "Yes, I know a father who made it an excuse too. But it isn't their fault. We can't make ourselves love someone just because we want to." (Chapter 4, Page 143)

Cordelia is speaking with Mrs. Goddard, who was nanny to Mark's mother. They are discussing what happens to children whose mothers die in childbirth. Cordelia is referencing her own father and excusing his behavior by saying that love can't be forced. If she believes this, she can see her father's rejection of her as impersonal. When she later confronts Sir Ronald, he says the same thing back to her, only in his case it's how he explains murdering his own son. If Cordelia's father did not love her and interrupted her education to serve as his cook and attendant, James wants us to consider how different he is from Sir Ronald, who tips over the edge into murder.

18. "Surely those two letters under an initial could only show one thing, the blood group." (Chapter 4, Page 156)

Cordelia has just discovered Evelyn's coded message to her son, Mark, in which she left her own initials, the letters "AA," and a date. This line is significant because it represents a tremendous intuitive leap. Correctly interpreting "AA" is key to solving the case; it is a stretch to imagine Cordelia immediately associating those two letters with a blood group.

19. "Thinking of her father and Bernie, Cordelia said: 'Perhaps it's only when people are dead that we can safely show how much we cared about them. We know that it's too late for them to do anything about it.'" (Chapter 4, Page 170)

On first read, these lines suggest that Cordelia cared for both her father and for Bernie Pryde, but a closer look shows that Cordelia could have been thinking about them in opposition. She cared very much for Bernie and not at all for her father, which gives these words a deeper resonance than initially suggested.

20. "Be sure of one thing, Miss Gray, if I needed to kill I should do it efficiently. I should not be found out. [...] Mark's death was necessary and, unlike most deaths, it served a purpose. Human beings have an irresistible urge towards self-sacrifice. They die for any reason or none at all, for meaningless abstractions like patriotism, justice, peace; for other men's ideas, for other men's power, for a few feet of earth." (Chapter 6, Page 198)

Sir Ronald has been found out, a fact he decides to ignore. His attempt at justifying Mark's death has some logic to it, but he fails to notice that Mark did not actually sacrifice himself—Sir Ronald sacrificed him. Miss Leaming does the same thing a few minutes later, sacrificing Sir Ronald, raising the moral ambiguity of who should be allowed to get away with murder.

21. "Intense personal commitment always ends in jealousy and enslavement. Love is more destructive than hate." (Chapter 6, Page 200)

*Sir Ronald has all but admitted to killing his own son,
explaining his actions were justified to protect his work.
In an ironic turn, Miss Leaming shows the truth of his
words when she kills him: Her intense personal
commitment to him and her love for her son leads her
to commit the same crime he committed, but for
opposite reasons.*

22. "Miss Leaming suddenly laughed and said with
    revealing bitterness: 'What is there to be frightened of?
    We shall be dealing only with men.'" (Chapter 6, Page
    209)

*On the surface Miss Leaming is deriding the way men
underestimate women. But she's also right; it is
unlikely a female police officer will be present. The
implication is that another woman might have found
them out, but the police will be hampered by their own
sexism in sending all men to investigate. That said,
James allows Dalgliesh to discover the truth. Since he
and Cordelia are both detectives, this reinforces the
trope that their intellect is superior to everyone's
regardless of gender.*

23. "Never tell an unnecessary lie; the truth has great
    authority. The cleverest murderers have been caught,
    not because they told the one essential lie, but because
    they continued to lie about unimportant details when
    the truth could have done them no harm." (Chapter 6,
    Page 219)

*Cordelia received this advice from Dalgliesh via Bernie
Pryde. It is ironic that Dalgliesh's guidance is exactly
what enables Cordelia to bluff him; it is also ironic that
a police officer is providing advice to a criminal.*

24. "If you're tempted to crime, stick to your original statement. There's nothing that impresses the jury more than consistency. I've seen the most unlikely defence succeed simply because the accused stuck to his story." (Chapter 7, Pages 244-45)

   Cordelia is recalling advice from Dalgliesh via Bernie, which she follows during her interrogation by Dalgliesh. This again raises the question why Dalgliesh gave advice about how to get away with criminal behavior when he is a police officer and why Bernie would pass on the same. The detective exists in a liminal space and creates his own morality.

25. "Most of all, she wished that she had someone to talk to about Ronald Callender's murder. Bernie wouldn't have been any help here. To him the moral dilemma at the heart of the crime would have held no interest, no validity, would have seemed a willful confusion of straightforward facts." (Chapter 7, Pages 245-46)

   Cordelia is on the verge of confessing to Dalgliesh that it was Miss Leaming who shot Sir Ronald. She is covering up this crime because she believes it would be immoral to punish Miss Leaming for killing the man who killed her son, but she has moments of doubt about this decision. By contrast, she thinks her old partner would have turned Miss Leaming in immediately, but still Cordelia sticks to her own concepts of right and wrong.

ESSAY TOPICS

1. James meant for Cordelia's gender to be a surprising subversion of expectations when the novel was published in 1972. How might Cordelia's gender function in the story if the novel was published today?

2. Several characters describe Mark to Cordelia in the course of her investigation. How do their descriptions of Mark's personality reflect on their characters versus his? What does this suggest about the role appearance plays in society?

3. Detectives often follow their own code of conduct and morality in this genre of fiction. Cordelia is no different. She adheres to her code and becomes an arbiter of justice. Describe Cordelia's code as presented in the novel. Does it bring true justice? Would you make the same choices? Why or why not?

4. Sir Ronald is initially described as having "that almost physical glow, akin to sexuality and undimmed by weariness of ill-health, of men who knew and enjoyed the realities of power" (40). Later, "[h]is face reminded [Cordelia] of faces seen grotesquely reflected in grubby train windows at night—cavernous, the bones stripped of flesh, eyes set in fathomless sockets—faces resurrected from the dead" (195). How does James use physical descriptions to reveal character? Are there characters who don't match their outward appearances?

5. What role do the Marklands play in this novel? Miss Markland in particular is an interesting character—what

do you make of her backstory, and what function does she serve?

6. Red herrings, or false clues, are a common trope in detective fiction. Where, how, and why does James plant red herrings in this story?

7. Several characters are orphaned or lose their mothers at a very young age. What purpose do all these dead mothers and fathers serve in the novel? Is there any relationship between a person's parentage and how they turn out?

8. Cordelia dreamed of attending Cambridge; instead she becomes a private detective who investigates the murder of a former Cambridge student. Do you think Cordelia regrets where her path has taken her? Why or why not, and how does James convey this in the text?

9. How does Cordelia Gray compare to male detective fiction protagonists like Adam Dalgleish, Sam Spade, and Philip Marlowe, to name a few?

10. Is *An Unsuitable Job for a Woman* a feminist novel? Defend your answer using evidence from the text and contemporary political events.

CPSIA information can be obtained
at www.ICGtesting.com
Printed in the USA
BVHW051403270223
659294BV00014B/585